The Christmas Redwood

Janice Kirk
Janice E. Kirk

WIPF & STOCK · Eugene, Oregon

Wipf and Stock Publishers
199 W 8th Ave, Suite 3
Eugene, OR 97401

The Christmas Redwood
A Forest Parable
By Kirk, Janice Emily
Copyright©2007 by Kirk, Janice Emily
ISBN 13: 978-1-5326-1200-8
Publication date 10/14/2016
Previously published by OakTara Publishers, 2007

*For Don,
Who took me there.*

"Grandfather, tell us the story again,
About the redwood tree."

Grandfather settles himself by the fire.

He smiles at the children, and then he begins…

Deep in the woods a stately old tree
Feels a change in the wind
And shakes out long limbs full of cones.

A seed is flung wide

And drops to the ground.

It is buried by wind in the duff and the dirt

Planted deep on that first Christmas night.

Glory to God,

Glory to God,

Glory to God in the highest.

The sheep hear the angels
And bleat out the news.

Wolf sings it aloft in the night.

When great love is given, the animals speak,

And the message spreads through the woods:

"A child is born,

"The Lamb of God."

The old tree nods, stretching out limbs

To protect the young sprout in the ground.

The lion prowls near

And inquires of the calf,

"Who is the Bethlehem child?"

And the word that comes back

In the quiet of dawn

Goes from creature to creature.

The old tree bends to the seedling.

"The Lord of Creation now walks the earth,

And all nature is waiting his blessing."

"Will he come to the woods?" asks leopard.

"Will he visit us here?" asks bear.

Then goat tells leopard,

"He's now a young boy,

He grows sturdy and strong

With laughter and joy.

The people love him,

All creatures too."

And the news travels fast through the woods.

Deep in the forest the young tree thrives.

With God's blessing of light

And life-giving rains,

It grows sturdy and strong by the guardian tree,

In a caring and sharing enclosure of love,

The fellowship of the forest.

Again comes news of Messiah
As cow tells bear, and bear passes it on—

"He is preaching and teaching,

He says, 'Follow me!'

And lost sheep are following

Throughout Galilee."

The young tree hears,

And leans with the wind,

Yearning to follow the Lord.

It murmurs the question for all of the woods,

"How can I?

I'm rooted right here."

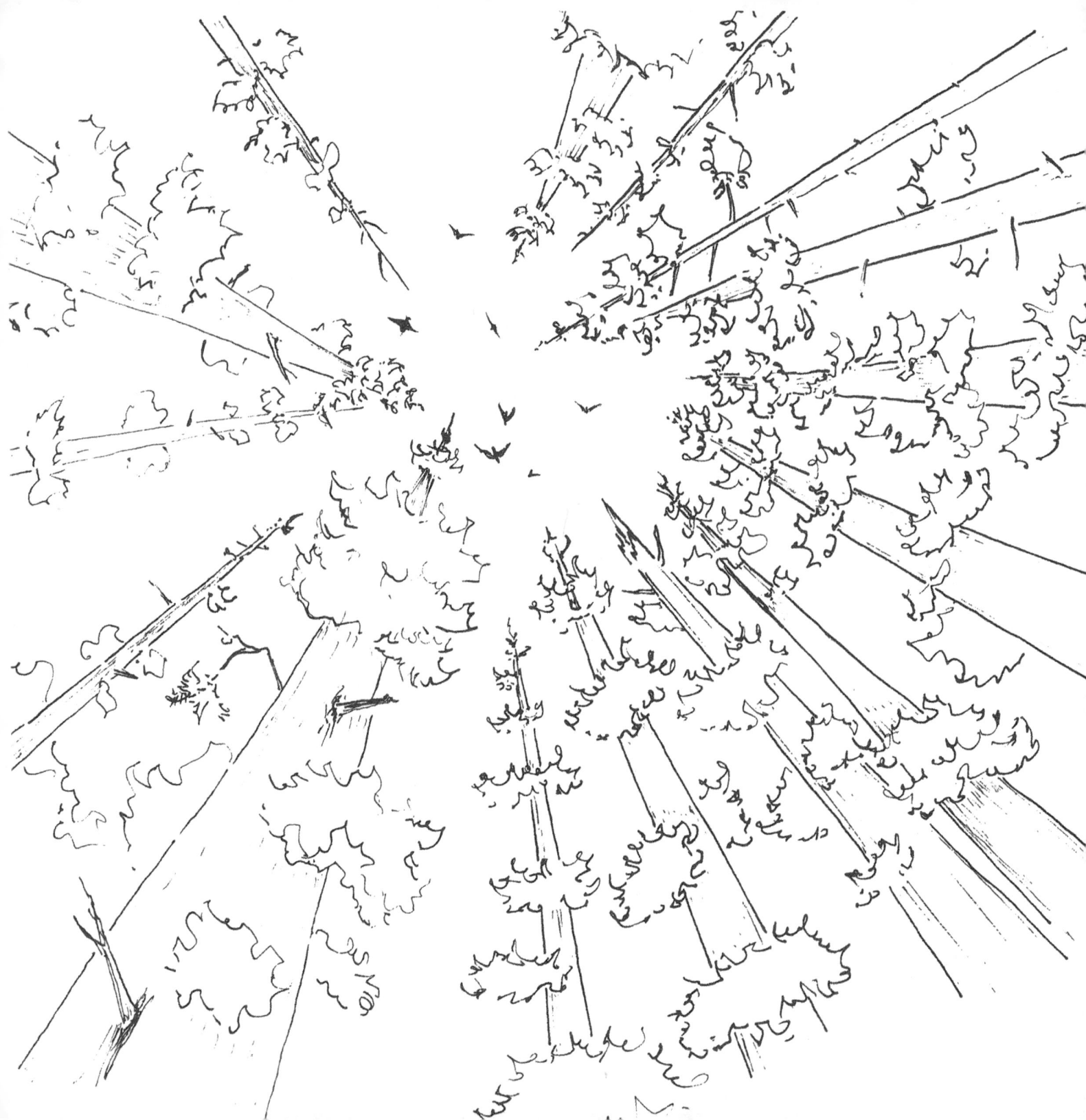

The birds of the air flutter close to the lake.

They listen, and then they report.

From creature to creature the lessons are passed

And the tree in the woods hears the teachings:

"Trust in God's Word,

It is right, it is true.

Love one another,

As I have loved you."

"Be sure to forgive,

Be willing to share.

My sheep need your help,

My meadows, your care.

Hold fast! For one day I'll return."

In silence the earth

Hears the charge, feels the joy!

The message gives hope,

Overflowing with love.

The tree claps its hands

As the hills burst with song.

God's creatures rejoice

As the wind of the Spirit sweeps over the land

And sets all nature to dancing.

Glory to God,

Glory to God,

Glory to God in the highest.

The tree holds fast by spreading out roots,

Intertwining with roots of its neighbors.

"This is my place to follow God's plan."

It freshens the air, makes food, and bears cones,

As it grows up tall in the forest.

In all of the storms and the wild ways of nature,
The tree in the woods stands its ground.

And the grain of the heartwood in inner dimension

Grows strong

    And is lasting.

        And true.

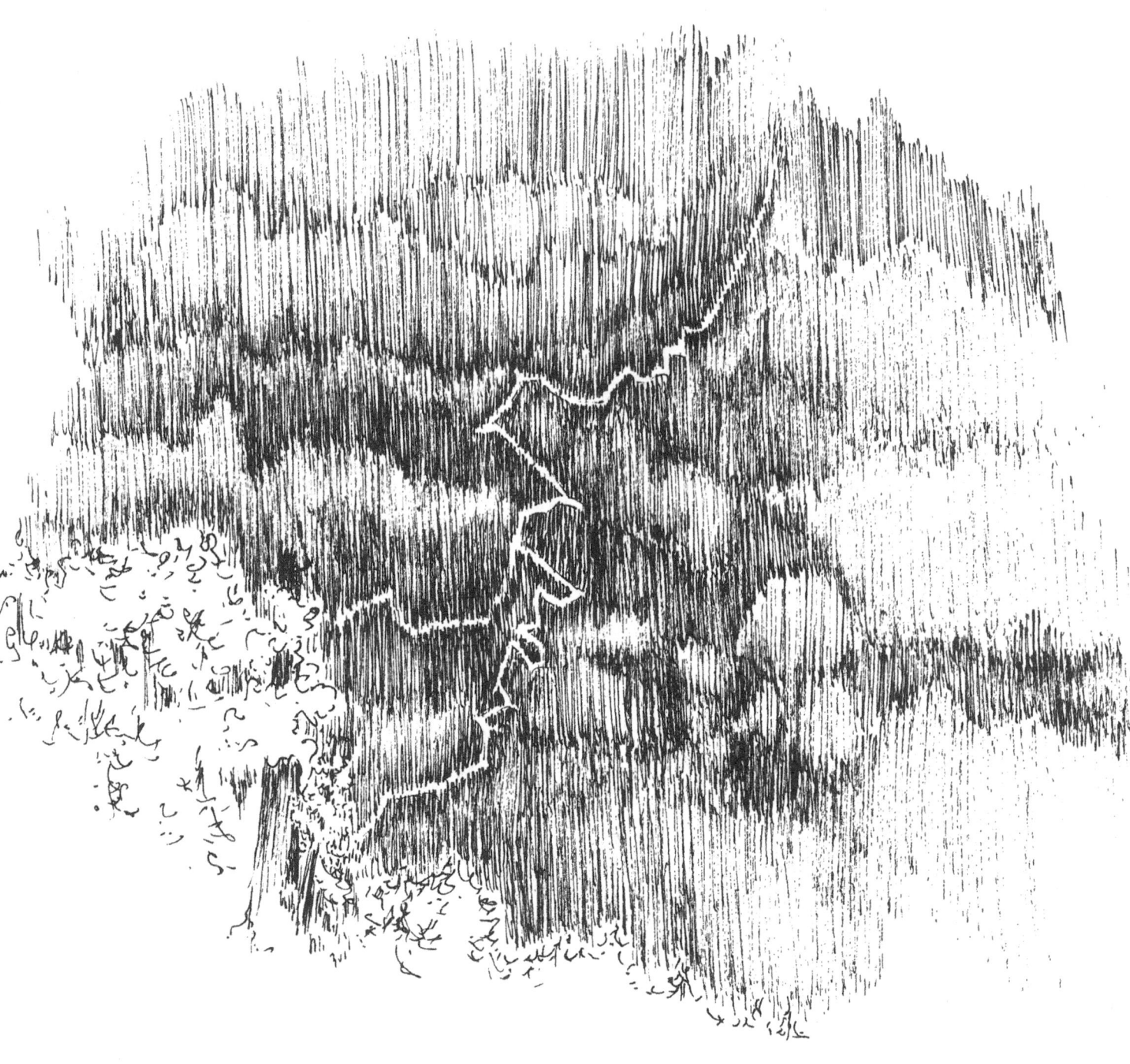

One day the sun stops shining

And darkness spreads over the land.

Clouds gather and threaten.

Earth quakes and rocks split.

A lightning bolt flashes out of the sky,

Striking the tree in the forest.

"What happened?" cries fox,
From his lair by the tree.

The eagle swoops low with sad news

Of the death of our Lord.

And the tree in the woods,

Where the branch split apart,

Shows the grain of the wood—

Like the blood of the Lamb,

It is found to be red to the heart.

Again comes the eagle, and fox spreads the word,
"Jesus rose from the dead, amazing his friends.
Now He's gone. He is risen to glory."

A groaning of loss arises from earth

But the redwood remembers the promise,

"Hold fast! For one day I'll return."

For one thousand years the seasons flow on.

The tree now stands as guardian.

"I shepherd no sheep,

Just these creatures of God,

Sharing life, giving life to each other."

Two thousand years pass, yet each Christmas Eve

A hush falls over the forest.

Expectant, God's creatures listen

For the voice of the Lamb

And the angel song.

Grandfather smiles at the children.

"Tonight, we wait with creation

On this blessed Eve that is set apart,

Like the ancient redwood that stands in the forest,

Let's hold fast and be faithful,

Be true and take heart."

Glory to God,

Glory to God,

Glory to God in the highest.

Fun Facts

- The oldest redwood is older than Christmas with 2200 counted tree rings.

- More than one tree is 2000 years old.

- Redwood trees reproduce through seeds and root crown sprouts.

- Winter storms toughen trees as they respond to wind and weather changes.

- Redwood bark lacks flammable resin and does not burn easily.

- Redwood bark is very thick, up to one foot on older trees.

- Redwood is a very straight-grained wood, strong and true.

- Redwood has wood that is red.

- A redwood grove is home to myriad plants and animals, a rich community of life.

- Less than 4% of the original ancient redwood forest remains today.

Helps for Parents and Teachers

In *The Christmas Redwood,* a redwood seed is planted by wind on the first Christmas night. The parable unfolds as animals spread the news of the Lord of Creation. The story of Jesus affects all nature. The tree grows and thrives, holding fast and sharing God's love in the forest. An example of faith and endurance, the tree still lives, waiting for Jesus to come again.
We all can learn to "hold fast and be faithful, be true and take heart."

Follow the story of Jesus:

- Birth
- Lord of Creation
- Teaching ministry
- Crucifixion
- Resurrection
- Promised return

Explore the teachings of Jesus:

- Love God
- Love one another
- Follow me
- Take care of my sheep
- Hold fast
- One day I'll return

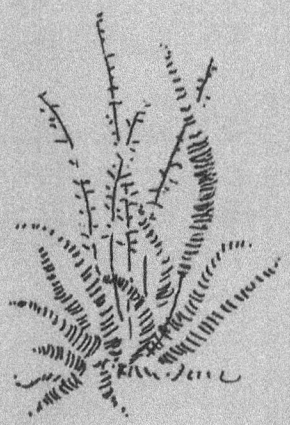

How to follow Jesus:

- Put down roots.
- Grow, bloom, and bear fruit where you are.
- Share the love.
- Do your part.

Questions & Answers:

- Can the animals talk? Yes, when great love is given.
    (Ps. 148:7-13; Isa. 11:6-9)

- Can trees clap their hands? Yes, when the wind of the Spirit sets them dancing.
    (Isa. 55:12)

- Do trees get hurt? Yes, but God heals all wounds and sets things aright.
    (Ps. 30:2; Isa. 53:5)

- Can the trees of the forest sing? Yes, they will sing for joy when the Lord comes.
    (Ps. 96:12-13)

- Can nature feel happy? Yes, it can shout for joy and sing.
    (Ps. 65:12-13)

About the Author

JANICE E. KIRK is a long-term arts educator, writer, and illustrator. She is co-author of *Cherish the Earth: The Environment and Scripture*, with Donald R. Kirk (Herald Press: 1993). She illustrated *Wild Edible Plants of Western North America*, by D. R. Kirk (Naturegraph: 1970). Janice has taught public school art, language arts, music, and gifted children. She is presently Adjunct Faculty at Simpson University. Semi-retirement has provided the time and opportunity to write about her many interests and her Christian faith. She is an advocate for responsible Earth Stewardship, a Christian concern.

With her biologist/naturalist husband, Don, and two children, Janice has traveled, camping, sketching, and photographing, all over the American West, including Redwood National Park. Over the years Janice has developed a unique and comprehensive viewpoint of the marvelous natural world, based on an artist's eye and outdoor experience. She loves to share camping stories and the fun of living close to nature. She writes and paints in hopes that others might see the glory of God through the window of his creation.

For more information about Janice E. Kirk:
www.kirksnaturebooks.net

www.ingramcontent.com/pod-product-compliance
Lightning Source LLC
Chambersburg PA
CBHW080554170426
43195CB00016B/2794